Do Your Ears
Hang
Low?

Do Your Ears Hang Low?

Fifty More Musical Fingerplays

Tom Glazer
Illustrated by Mila Lazarevich

290912
Doubleday & Company, Inc., Garden City, New York

Library of Congress Cataloging in Publication Data

Glazer, Tom.
  Do your ears hang low?

  SUMMARY: Presents words and music to 50 songs
with directions for accompanying fingerplays.
  1. Singing games. 2. Children's songs.
[1. Singing games. 2. Songs] I. Lazarevich, Mila.
II. Title.
M1993.G54D6 [M1997]   784.6′24′06
Library of Congress Catalog Card Number 78–20072
          ISBN: 0-385-12602-6 Trade
          ISBN: 0-385-12603-4 Prebound

Acknowledgments

Piano arrangements by Tom Glazer.

All songs herein are adapted and collected, with original lyrics and/or music added in part or wholly, by Tom Glazer, and are copyrighted by Songs Music, Inc., Scarborough, N.Y. 10510. They are reprinted by permission.

Music typography by Irwin Rabinowitz and Saul Honigman.

Introduction

This book has come about because of the kind reception by educators and the general public of my first book of musical fingerplays, *Eye Winker, Tom Tinker, Chin Chopper . . . 50 Musical Fingerplays,* Doubleday, 1973. What I said, in part, in my introduction to that work applies here as well. I said that Friedrich Froebel, father of the kindergarten (1782–1852), wrote, "What the child imitates, he (she) begins to understand. Let him represent the flying of birds and he enters partially into the life of the birds. Let him imitate the rapid motion of fishes in the water and his sympathy with fishes is quickened. . . . In a word let him reflect in his play the varied aspects of life and his thoughts will begin to grapple with their significance."

I went on to say that Froebel had actually collected fingerplays in the field from peasant mothers, as folklorists do, along with other games mothers played with their children, which interested me as a folk singer, and that the earliest fingerplay books in the United States, like Emilie Poulsson's *Finger Plays for Nursery and Kindergarten* (1893), which had gone to over 90,000 copies, had contained, invariably, music for the fingerplays.

Gradually, though, fingerplay music had virtually died out. Probably, I surmised, because piano playing by teachers of the young had become impractical, so that most recent fingerplay books contained little or no music.

In *"Eye Winker . . ."* I used existing fingerplay songs, and had adapted other songs to this end, or had set fingerplay lyrics to music. This is what I have done in this book as well. Some of the songs are very well known, either as fingerplays or nursery songs; others are either unfamiliar or have never appeared in print before; it is always a very great pleasure for performers to pass along to the public delicious songs they have come by one way or another or have adapted, arranged or shaped themselves.

The songs in this book are fun and often very funny. Children adore humor, even zaniness, as well as fancy, fable and fantasy, the basic "F's," I think, of their creative lives, so that I know of no better way to get educational ideas across than through these devices of enchantment. It has been pointed out so wisely that learning can be accomplished in two major ways: through fear or through love.

It is a pleasure to thank Kim Hamilton and Carol Greco for their help with some of the material. I must thank, too, the Girl Scouts of America, whose singing tradition is tasteful, long and valuable. The experience, wisdom and help of my editor, Janet Chenery, is beyond thanks.

Tom Glazer
Scarborough, New York
1976–77

Suggestions on Use of the Songs

Guitar, banjo, Autoharp or similar accompanying instruments may be used if the piano isn't available; chords are supplied. Use the *capo* or transpose to a simpler, adjoining, key if necessary.

Dynamic markings were deliberately kept to a minimum. Most of the songs are obvious enough as to speed to require no metronomic strictures; this is also true of loudness or softness. Play the songs according to your own feelings.

The songs are arranged alphabetically for easy locating. The children may or may not sing them while acting them out at the discretion of the song leader, though singing all or part of them is more fun as a rule.

Above all, try to be flexible; change or shorten or improvise as the spirit moves you. Add, subtract, multiply or divide, and become part of the "folk process," an ancient and honorable tradition in which individual creativity takes what is given and shapes and alters and passes it along to the next generation to use and reshape or keep intact. This is what every great artist has done in any field, but this has also been done by anonymous unself-conscious thousands through the centuries, in smaller ways perhaps, but nonetheless just as movingly and often as brilliantly.

Contents

For John and Deedee and their children

Do Your Ears
Hang
Low?

1. Ain't It Great to Be Kooky

Moderately

Chorus

Zoom! Zoom! Ain't it great to be koo - ky, Zoom! Zoom! Ain't it great to be

nuts, Dad-dle-de-a - da, Hap-py and gay, The whole darn day, Zoom!

Zoom! Ain't it great to be koo - ky. 1. I wish I was a lit-tle cake of

soap,   I wish I was a lit-tle cake of soap,   I'd slip-py and I'd slide ov-er

ev-'ry-bod-y's hide, I wish I was a lit-tle cake of soap.

2. I wish I was a little stripèd skunk,
I wish I was a little stripèd skunk,
I'd sit in all the treeses,
And perfume all the breezes,
I wish I was a little stripèd skunk.
Chorus:

3. I wish I was a can of Seven-up,
I wish I was a can of Seven-up,
I'd go down with a slurp,
And come up with a burp,
I wish I was a can of Seven-up.
Chorus:

4. I wish I was a fishie in the sea,
I wish I was a fishie in the sea,
I'd swim around so cute,
Without my bathing suit,
I wish I was a fishie in the sea.
Chorus:

5. I wish I was a buzzie old mosquito,
I wish I was a buzzie old mosquito,
I'd buzzie and I'd bitie,
Under everybody's nightie,
I wish I was a buzzie old mosquito.
Chorus:

Chorus: Hold arms up in front of face, palms out. On first "zoom," raise
both arms. On second "zoom," lower to original position in front
of face. During remainder of chorus hold arms and hands in same
position while moving upper part of body including head and
arms from side to side in time to music.

v. 1: Pretend to hold a cake of soap and soap yourself all over.

v. 2: Hold heel of right hand on top of left hand, with two fingers of right
hand and thumb held up. Bend these fingers up and down in rhythm.

v. 3: Pretend to drink out of a can or bottle, with one fist. Say "slurp" on
the word "slurp," and "burp" on the word "burp," then drink out of
"can" until end of verse.

v. 4: "Swim" with one hand, palm down in wavy motions all through verse.

v. 5: Place hands on ears, thumbs touching ears, fingers spread out. Wave
fingers in this position while making a buzzing sound.

(Chorus comes after every verse as above.)

1

2. The Ants Go Marching

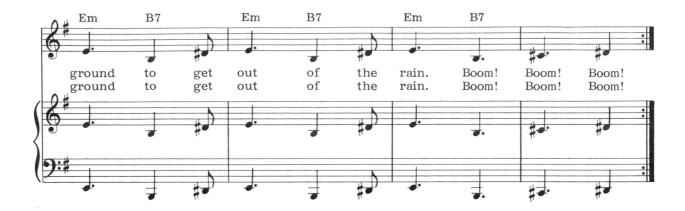

ground   to   get   out   of   the   rain.   Boom!   Boom!   Boom!

3. The ants go marching three by three, Hurrah, Hurrah,
   The ants go marching three by three, Hurrah, Hurrah,
   The ants go marching three by three; The little one stops to climb a tree, and they
   all go marching down into the ground to get out of the rain. Boom! Boom! Boom!

4. The ants go marching four by four, Hurrah, Hurrah,
   The ants go marching four by four, Hurrah, Hurrah,
   The ants go marching four by four; The little one stops to shut the door, and they
   all go marching down into the ground to get out of the rain. Boom! Boom! Boom!

5. The ants go marching five by five, Hurrah, Hurrah,
   The ants go marching five by five, Hurrah, Hurrah,
   The ants go marching five by five; The little one stops to take a dive, and they
   all go marching down into the ground to get out of the rain. Boom! Boom! Boom!

6. The ants go marching six by six, Hurrah, Hurrah,
   The ants go marching six by six, Hurrah, Hurrah,
   The ants go marching six by six; The little one stops to pick up sticks, and they
   all go marching down into the ground to get out of the rain. Boom! Boom! Boom!

7. The ants go marching seven by seven, Hurrah, Hurrah,
   The ants go marching seven by seven, Hurrah, Hurrah,
   The ants go marching seven by seven; The little one stops to pray to heaven, and they
   all go marching down into the ground to get out of the rain. Boom! Boom! Boom!

8. The ants go marching eight by eight, Hurrah, Hurrah,
   The ants go marching eight by eight, Hurrah, Hurrah,
   The ants go marching eight by eight; The little one stops to close the gate, and they
   all go marching down into the ground to get out of the rain. Boom! Boom! Boom!

9. The ants go marching nine by nine, Hurrah, Hurrah,
   The ants go marching nine by nine, Hurrah, Hurrah,
   The ants go marching nine by nine; The little one stops to spend a dime, and they
   all go marching down into the ground to get out of the rain. Boom! Boom! Boom!

10. The ants go marching ten by ten, Hurrah, Hurrah,
    The ants go marching ten by ten, Hurrah, Hurrah,
    The ants go marching ten by ten; The little one stops to say,
    Shouted: "THE END."

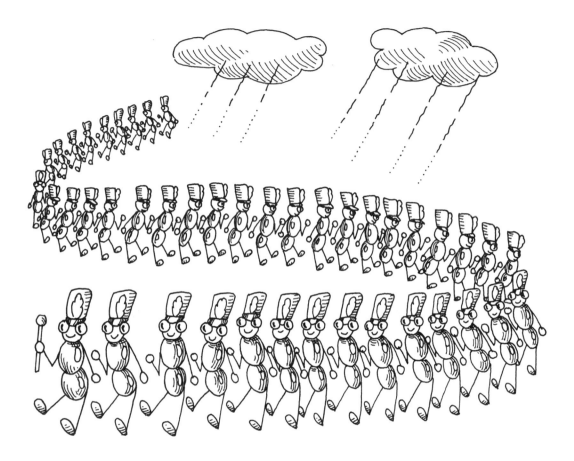

v. 1: With first two fingers of one hand, "march" up your other arm. At ". . . the little one stops to shoot his gun . . ." pretend to shoot a rifle with both hands, one arm outstretched, the other bent against the face. Then march down the arm with your two fingers, keeping arm pointed down to the ground.

v. 2: March with two fingers of both hands in the air as you move them forward before you. At ". . . tie his shoe . . ." pretend to tie your shoe.

v. 3 through 10: Do as indicated. In verse 9, pretend to give someone a dime. In verse 10, shout, "the end!"

3. Bottle Pop

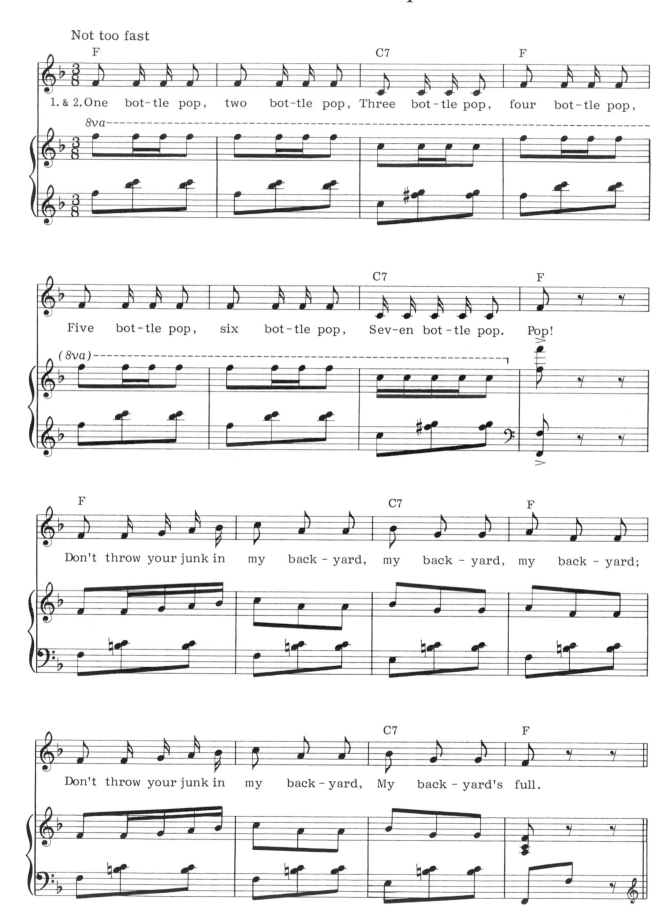

Raise the required number of fingers as each number is sung. On the word
"pop," either clap or, if you can, make a pop sound in the traditional way by
pulling a finger out of the side of your mouth suddenly.

Chorus: Shake an admonishing finger in rhythm through the word "full."
At ". . . fish and chips . . ." make swimming motion with one
hand. At the last "pop" make same pop sound or loud clap.

4. Bow Belinda

1. Bow, bow, bow Be-lin-da; Bow, bow, bow Be-lin-da; Bow, bow, bow Be-lin-da; Won't you be my dar-ling.

2. Right hand up, Oh Belinda;
Right hand up, Oh Belinda;
Right hand up, Oh Belinda;
Won't you be my darling.

3. Left hand up, Oh Belinda;
Left hand up, Oh Belinda;
Left hand up, Oh Belinda;
Won't you be my darling.

4. Both hands up, Oh Belinda;
Both hands up, Oh Belinda;
Both hands up, Oh Belinda;
Won't you be my darling.

5. Right foot out, Oh Belinda;
Right foot out, Oh Belinda;
Right foot out, Oh Belinda;
Won't you be my darling.

6. Left foot out, Oh Belinda;
Left foot out, Oh Belinda;
Left foot out, Oh Belinda;
Won't you be my darling.

7. Hug yourself, Oh Belinda;
Hug yourself, Oh Belinda;
Hug yourself, Oh Belinda;
Won't you be my darling.

8. Blow a kiss, Oh Belinda;
Blow a kiss, Oh Belinda;
Blow a kiss, Oh Belinda;
Won't you be my darling.

Suit the action to the words. Substitute for Belinda the name of any child in the group. That child does the bowing by him- or herself.

5. Buddies and Pals

3. You and me, we're born to be friendly.
   You and me, we're born to have fun.
   You and me, we're born to be friendly,
   Friendly and fun.

4. You and me, are gonna get with it.
   You and me, are gonna get close.
   You and me, are gonna get with it,
   With it and close.

10

Pair off the children. Touch palms of hands to palms of partner on word "you." Touch palms against own chest on word "me." Shake hands on the phrases ". . . are gonna be partners . . . ," ". . . are gonna be pals . . . ," and on "buddies and pals." Same pattern in all verses.

6. Bye Baby Bunting

1. Bye, Ba-by Bunt-ing, Dad-dy's gone a-hunt-ing, To get a lit-tle rab-bit skin, To wrap his ba-by bunt-ing in.
2. Bye, Ba-by Bunt-ing, Mam-my's gone a-hunt-ing, To find a lit-tle safe-ty pin, To fast-en ba-by's dia-per in.

v. 1, line 1: Wave bye-bye. l. 2: Hold imaginary rifle, one arm extended, the other bent with fist under the eye. l. 3: Hold arms up before face, hands bent a little, "holding a skin." l. 4: Rock a baby in your arms.

v. 2: Wave bye-bye. Hold rifle. Open and close a forefinger against its thumb. Pat pretend baby.

7. Can You Plant a Cabbage?

14

2. Can you pick a cabbage, dear?
   Can you pick it? Can you pick it?
   Can you pick a cabbage, dear?
   Just the way we pick it here.

3. Can you eat a cabbage, dear?
   Can you eat it? Can you eat it?
   Can you eat a cabbage, dear?
   Just the way we eat it here.

4. Sauerkraut is cabbage, dear.
   Did you know it? Did you know it?
   Sauerkraut is cabbage, dear.
   It's so tart, you'll shed a tear.

5. Can you plant a cabbage, dear?
   Can you plant it? Can you plant it?
   Can you plant a cabbage, dear?
   Just the way we plant it here.

v. 1: Point to ground, with rest of hand closed, in time to music.
v. 2: Make a pulling motion throughout verse.
v. 3: Chew throughout verse.
v. 4: Hold one hand out vertically and make a chopping motion.
Repeat verse 1.

8. Clapping Land

1. I trav - elled ov - er land and sea; I met a man and old was he. "Old man," I said, "where do you live?" And this is what he told me:

Fol - low me to clap-ping land, All who want to live with me.
All who want to live with me, Fol - low me to clap-ping land.

2. I travelled over land and sea;
   I met a man and old was he.
   "Old man, "I said, "where do you live?"
   And this is what he told me:
   Follow me to stamping land,
   All who want to live with me.
   All who want to live with me,
   Follow me to stamping land.

4. I travelled over land and sea;
   I met a man and old was he.
   "Old man," I said, "where do you live?"
   And this is what he told me:
   Follow me to skipping land,
   All who want to live with me.
   All who want to live with me,
   Follow me to skipping land.

16

3. I travelled over land and sea;
   I met a man and old was he.
   "Old man," I said, "where do you live?"
   And this is what he told me:
   Follow me to hopping land,
   All who want to live with me.
   All who want to live with me,
   Follow me to hopping land.

6. I travelled over land and sea;
   I met a man and old was he.
   "Old man," I said, "where do you live?"
   And this is what he told me:
   Follow me to nodding land,
   All who want to live with me.
   All who want to live with me,
   Follow me to nodding land.

7. I travelled over land and sea;
   I met a man and old was he.
   "Old man," I said, "where do you live?"
   And this is what he told me:
   Follow me to tiptoe land,
   All who want to live with me.
   All who want to live with me,
   Follow me to tiptoe land.

5. I travelled over land and sea;
   I met a man and old was he.
   "Old man," I said, "where do you live?"
   And this is what he told me:
   Follow me to pointing land,
   All who want to live with me.
   All who want to live with me,
   Follow me to pointing land.

8. I travelled over land and sea;
   I met a man and old was he.
   "Old man," I said, "where do you live?"
   And this is what he told me:
   Follow me to handshake land,
   All who want to live with me.
   All who want to live with me,
   Follow me to handshake land.

9. Make one up.

10. Make another one up.

Verse: Clap on first beat of each measure, once in each bar.
Chorus 1: Clap twice in each bar, on first and third beats.
Other Choruses: Do what they say to do. (The verse is always the same.)

9. The Crocodile

She sailed a - way, on a hap-py sum-mer day, On the back of a croc - o -
dile. "You'll see," said she, "he's as tame as tame can be; I'll
ride him down the Nile." The croc winked his eye, as she
bade them all good-bye, Wear-ing a hap - py smile. At the

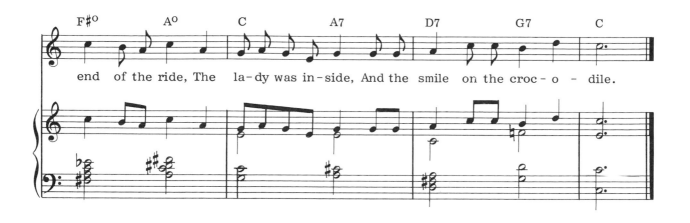

end of the ride, The la-dy was in-side, And the smile on the croc-o - dile.

"She sailed away . . ." place palm on back of other hand with both thumbs extended to side. Make rowing motion with thumbs and wavy motion with hands at the same time as hands move forward. (It's not hard.)

". . . on the back of a crocodile . . ." clap three times in rhythm.

". . . you'll see, said she . . ." shake admonishing finger in rhythm.

". . . I'll ride him down the Nile . . ." same as line 1.

". . . winked his eye . . ." wink.

". . . bade them all good-bye . . ." wave.

". . . wearing a happy smile . . ." smile.

". . . end of the ride . . ." same as line 1.

". . . the lady was inside . . ." pat belly.

". . . and the smile on the crocodile" same as line 1, except spread fingers and don't row with thumbs.

10. Dewy

Dew - ey was a cap - tain at Man - il - a bay.

Dew - y was a morn - ing, in the month of May.

Dew - y were her lips as she pledged her love a - new.

Do we love each oth - er? Yes, in - deed, we do.

line 1: Salute.
   l. 2: Lace fingers and hold hands over head like an umbrella.
   l. 3: Kissing sound.
   l. 4: Hug yourselves.

11. Do Your Ears Hang Low?

3. Do your ears hang high?
   Do they stand up in the sky?
   Do they drop down when they're wet?
   Do they stand up when they're dry?
   Do you wave them to your neighbor,
   With a minimum of labor?
   Do your ears hang high?

4. Yes, my ears hang high,
   And they stand up in the sky;
   And they drop down when they're wet,
   And they stand up when they're dry;
   And I wave them to my neighbor,
   With a minimum of labor.
   Yes, my ears hang high.

v. 1 and 2: Pull down on your ear lobes three times, on "ears," "hang,"
and "low." Then wobble them to and fro. Then make twisty motion
with both fists, as in tying something. Then throw over your shoulder.
Then end as you began by pulling your lobes three times on the same
words.

v. 3 and 4: Pull ear lobes upward on first two lines. Pull lobes down. Pull
ears up holding them from the top. Hold one ear and shake it through
lines four and five. Last line same as line one.

12. The Donut Song

1. Oh, I walked a-round the cor-ner, And I walked a-round the block, And I
2. Well, she looked at the nick-el, And she looked at me, And she

walked right in - to a bake-ry shop, And I picked up a
said, "Hey, mis-ter can't you plain - ly see? There's a hole in the

do-nut, and I wiped off the grease, And I hand - ed the la - dy a
nick-el, there's a hole right through." Said I, "There's a hole in the

five cent piece.
do - nut too!"

Thanks for the do - nut-- Good day!"

v. 1, lines 1 and 2: Describe circle horizontally with your forefinger in front of you. l. 3: Open "door." l. 4: Pick up donut and wipe. l. 5: Hand lady a nickel.

v. 2, line 1: Place hands on hips and stare at someone up and down. l. 2: ". . . can't you plainly see . . ." throw arms out, palms up. l. 3: Make a hole several times to end of verse. l. 4: ". . . thanks for the donut, good day" place fingertips against side of forehead and throw arm out in a "so-long" gesture.

13. Georgie

stick out my head, and go oo - oo - oo - oo - ooh, to Georg - ie.___

line 1: Look at your "wrist watch."

l. 2: On all the "ooh's" place hands in front of face, palms out, and move in circles.

l. 3: On "knock," rap a knuckle against your head.

l. 4: On "ring," imitate bell, vocally or manually.

l. 5: Rub your eyes, open the window, and stick out your head, and on the rest of the "ooh's," repeat as above in 2.

14. Ha! Ha! This-a-Way

Ha! Ha! This-a-way, Ha! Ha! That-a-way, Ha! Ha! This-a-way, then, oh, then.

1. When I was a lit-tle boy, lit-tle boy, lit-tle boy,
   Ma - ma used to scold___ me, scold___ me, scold___ me,

   When I was a lit-tle boy, Five years old.
   Ma - ma used to scold___ me, then, oh, then.

2. When I was a little girl, little girl, little girl,
   When I was a little girl, then, oh, then,
   Papa used to hold me, hold me, hold me,
   Papa used to hold me, then, oh, then.

Chorus: Ha! Ha! This-a-way, Ha! Ha! That-a-way, Ha! Ha! This-a-way, then, oh, then.

28

Chorus: Point four times in rhythm with one hand, then with the other, alternating through chorus.

v. 1: Hold one arm straight down, palm horizontal, moving arm three times on "little boy." At ". . . mama used to scold me . . ." point admonishing finger in rhythm.

v. 2: Same as 1, except hold baby on "hold me," rocking in rhythm.

15. Head, Shoulders, Knees, and Toes

Just point to each part of the body as it is mentioned.

16. Hello Song

2. Hello! Let's play some games. *(fun ones!)*
Hello! I love ice cream. *(yum, yum!)*
Hello! Your mom is pretty as anything.
Don't eat too much candy.

3. Hello! I washed my hands. *(with soap!)*
Hello! I washed my face. *(without soap)*
Hello! I thank you for your present.
I'm glad today's my birthday.

v. 1, line 1: Raise one hand up and wiggle fingers, then remove a pretend hat. l. 2: Wiggle fingers and remove coat. l. 3: Point to shoes and stockings and shake head, "no." l. 4: ". . . you came . . ." point to someone, ". . . to my party" point to yourself.

v. 2, line 1: Wiggle fingers on "hello," then make circles with both hands in front. l. 2: Wiggle fingers and pretend to eat ice cream. l. 3: Hold one hand to side of face and shake head, as if "wow!" l. 4: Point finger at someone and look stern.

v. 3, line 1: Washing motion with hands. l. 2: Wash face. l. 3: Shake hands with yourself. l. 4: Raise both hands, fists closed, and move them in a "ray, team!" motion.

17. Here We Go Looby Loo

1. Here we go Loo - by Loo,_____ Here we go Loo - by Light,_____ Here we go Loo - by Loo_____ All on a Sat - ur - day night._____ night._____

I put my right hand in; I put my right hand out; I

give my hand a shake, shake, shake, And turn my-self a - bout. Oh!

2. Here we go Looby Loo,
   Here we go Looby Light,
   Here we go Looby Loo,
   All on a Saturday night.

   I put my left hand in;
   I put my left hand out;
   I give my hand a shake, shake, shake,
   And turn myself about. Oh!

3. Here we go Looby Loo,
   Here we go Looby Light,
   Here we go Looby Loo,
   All on a Saturday night.

   I put my right foot in;
   I put my right foot out;
   I give my foot a shake, shake, shake,
   And turn myself about. Oh!

4. Here we go Looby Loo,
   Here we go Looby Light,
   Here we go Looby Loo,
   All on a Saturday night.

   I put my left foot in;
   I put my left foot out;
   I give my foot a shake, shake, shake,
   And turn myself about. Oh!

5. Here we go Looby Loo,
   Here we go Looby Light,
   Here we go Looby Loo,
   All on a Saturday night.

   I put my whole self in;
   I put my whole self out;
   I give myself a shake, shake, shake,
   And turn myself about. Oh!

Last time:

   Here we go Looby Loo,
   Here we go Looby Light,
   Here we go Looby Loo,
   All on a Saturday night.

Chorus: Place hands on waist and wave from side to side in rhythm.
Verses: Do what they tell you to do.

18. The Hokey Pokey

1. You put your right foot in; You take your right foot out; You put your right foot in, And you shake it all a-bout; You do the Hok-ey Pok-ey, and you turn your-self a-bout. That's what it's all a - bout.____

2. You put your left foot in;
   You take your left foot out;
   You put your left foot in;
   And you shake it all about;
   You do the Hokey Pokey,
   And you turn yourself about.
   That's what it's all about.

3. You put your right hand in;
   You take your right hand out;
   You put your right hand in,
   And you shake it all about;
   You do the Hokey Pokey,
   And you turn yourself about.
   That's what it's all about.

4. You put your left hand in;
   You take your left hand out;
   You put your left hand in;
   And you shake it all about;
   You do the Hokey Pokey,
   And you turn yourself about.
   That's what it's all about.

5. You put your right shoulder in;
   You take your right shoulder out;
   You put your right shoulder in,
   And you shake it all about;
   You do the Hokey Pokey,
   And you turn yourself about.
   That's what it's all about.

6. You put your left shoulder in;
   You take your left shoulder out;
   You put your left shoulder in,
   And you shake it all about;
   You do the Hokey Pokey,
   And you turn yourself about.
   That's what it's all about.

7. You put your right hip in;
   You take your right hip out;
   You put your right hip in,
   And you shake it all about;
   You do the Hokey Pokey,
   And you turn yourself about.
   That's what it's all about.

8. You put your left hip in;
   You take your left hip out;
   You put your left hip in,
   And you shake it all about;
   You do the Hokey Pokey,
   And you turn yourself about.
   That's what it's all about.

9. You put your whole self in;
   You take your whole self out;
   You put your whole self in,
   And you shake it all about;
   You do the Hokey Pokey,
   And you turn yourself about.
   That's what it's all about.

(*Note:* This a traditional round dance, very simple to do. The actions are the usual ones, but they can be adapted to finger/body play with children seated instead of standing, by twisting the body from side to side instead of turning completely about. Do it either way.)

   line 1: Put a foot forward, or any body part indicated, then return foot, or other body part.
   l. 2: Put forward again and shake it.
   l. 3: Turn about in four steps or twist body to side and back, with hands up and fingers wiggling.
   l. 4: Clap four times on last line, "That's what it's all about."

36

19. The Horse Stood Around

Chorus:

1. Oh, the horse stood a-round with his foot on the ground-- The

horse stood a-round with his foot on the ground; The horse stood a-round with his

foot on the ground-- The horse stood a-round with his foot on the ground.*

Coda (after last chorus)

The Old Gray Mare, she ain't what she used to be!

After chorus say: "Same horse, second foot, then repeat.

2. Oh, the horse stood around with his foot on the ground--
   The horse stood around with his foot on the ground;
   The horse stood around with his foot on the ground--
   The horse stood around with his foot on the ground.

Spoken: "Same horse, third foot *(then repeat)*

3. Oh, the horse stood around with his foot on the ground--
   The horse stood around with his foot on the ground;
   The horse stood around with his foot on the ground--
   The horse stood around with his foot on the ground.

Spoken: "Same horse, fourth foot *(then repeat)*

4. Oh, the horse stood around with his foot on the ground--
   The horse stood around with his foot on the ground;
   The horse stood around with his foot on the ground--
   The horse stood around with his foot on the ground.

Spoken: "Same horse, fifth foot *(to Coda)*

Coda: The Old Gray Mare, she ain't what she used to be!

Tramp with right foot in time to music but not during spoken part. On "the old gray mare . . ." stick your tongue out, put your thumbs in your ears and wiggle your fingers.
Tramp with left foot during 2nd chorus; the rest stays the same.
Alternate feet during 3rd chorus.
Both feet at once in the 4th chorus.
On 5th chorus, stand on one foot if you can; if you can't, stand on no feet.

20. Hold Up Your Petticoats

(Girls) 1. Hold up your pet-ti-coats, dance like a la-dy, No-bod-y home but ma-ma and the ba-by. Hold up your pet-ti-coats, dance like a la-dy, No-bod-y home but ma-ma and the ba-by.

(Boys) 2. Hitch up your blue-jeans, dance with a lady,

Nobody home but mama and the baby.

Hold up your blue-jeans, dance with a lady,

Nobody home but mama and the baby.

(Both) 3. Bow to your partner, dance {like a / with a} lady,

Nobody home but mama and the baby.

Bow to your partner, dance {like a / with a} lady,

Nobody home but mama and the baby.

39

v. 1: Girls hike up jeans or skirts a little and swing your feet if seated, or do a dance step if standing. Same on line 3. Rock a baby, lines 2 and 4.

v. 2, lines 1 and 3: Boys hitch up jeans or pants, then slap neighbor's hand with your own. lines 2 and 4: Rock a baby.

v. 3: Everyone bow to a neighbor, then slap that neighbor's hand with yours, lines 1 and 3. lines 2 and 4: Rock baby.

21. I Had a Little Nut Tree

I had a lit-tle nut tree, noth-ing it would bear, But a sil-ver nut-meg and a gold-en pear. The King of Spain's daught-er came to vis-it me, And all for the sake of my lit-tle nut tree.

41

line 1: Form a tree by raising both hands to touch fingers over head, then
bring down gracefully, and shake head, "no," on ". . . nothing
it would bear . . ."

l. 2: Raise fist for nutmeg and other fist for pear.

l. 3: Hand on head, fingers up and spread, as a crown.

l. 4: Make tree shape again.

22. I Had a Little Rooster

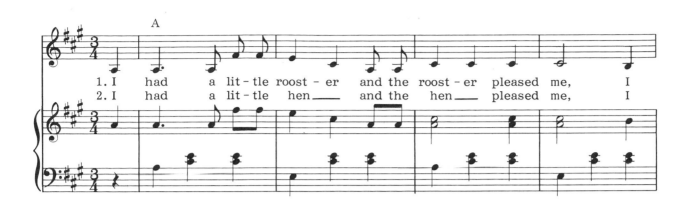

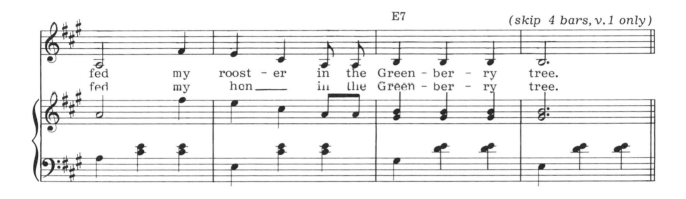

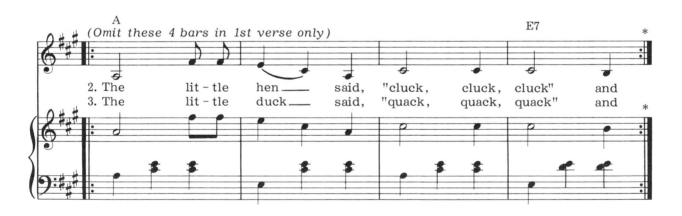

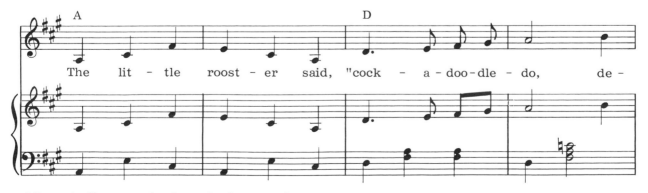

Repeat all verses backwards then continue to end.

doo - dle, de - doo - dle, de - doo - dle - de - doo."

3. I had a little duck and the duck pleased me,
   I fed my little duck in the Greenberry tree.
   The little duck said, "quack, quack, quack" and
   the little hen said, "cluck, cluck, cluck" and
   the little rooster said, "cock-a-doo-dle-do,
   de-doo-dle, de-doo-dle, de-doo-dle de-doo."

4. I had a little dog and the dog pleased me,
   I fed my dog in the Greenberry tree.
   The little dog said, "bow-wow-wow" and
   the little duck said, "quack, quack, quack" and
   the little hen said, "cluck, cluck, cluck" and
   the little rooster said, "cock-a-doo-dle-do,
   de-doo-dle, de-doo-dle, de-doo-dle de-doo."

v. 1, line 1: Raise right hand and wiggle fingers, then hug yourself. l. 2:
     Hold out the same hand, then point up. l. 3: Raise hand again and
     wiggle fingers to end.
v. 2: The same as before but with the left hand.
v. 3: Quack and swim with one hand, then do as in verses 1 and 2 for prior
     animals.
v. 4: Hold two fingers up for a dog, then do as before.

23. I Have Lost the "Do"

1. I have lost the 'do' of my cla – ri – net.___ I have lost the
'do' of my cla – ri – net.___ Oh, if dad-dy found me out, la, la,
la–– He would sure-ly chew me out, la, la, la. Let's
sing, sing, sing; Let's sing, sing, sing; Let's sing a lit – tle song. Let's

45

sing, sing, sing; Let's sing, sing, sing; Let's sing a lit - tle song.

2. I have lost the 're' of my violin.
   I have lost the 're' of my violin.
   And if mama found me out, la, la, la--
   On my head I'd get a clout, la, la, la.

   Chorus:

3. I have lost the 'mi' of my piccolo.
   I have lost the 'mi' of my piccolo.
   And if sister found me out, la, la, la--
   She would pull my great big snout, la, la, la.

   Chorus:

4. I have lost the 'fa' of my golden trumpet.
   I have lost the 'fa' of my golden trumpet.
   And if brother found me out, la, la, la--
   He would swear and stomp and shout, la, la, la.

   Chorus:

5. I have lost the 'sol' of my rock guitar.
   I have lost the 'sol' of my rock guitar.
   And if teacher found me out, la, la, la--
   He would chase me all about, la, la, la.

   Chorus:

6. I have lost the 'la' of my slide trombone.
   I have lost the 'la' of my slide trombone.
   And if grandma found me out, la, la, la--
   She would frown and cry and pout, la, la, la.

   Chorus:

7. I have lost the 'ti' of my big bass drum.
   I have lost the 'ti' of my big bass drum.
   And if grandpa found me out, la, la, la--
   He would feed me sauerkraut, la, la, la.

   Chorus:

8. If you find my 'do' won't you please return it.
   You'll get a reward, and I know you'll earn it.
   If you do you'll set me free.
   From my whole darn family.

   Chorus:

Simply imitate playing each instrument mentioned in verses 1 through 7.
v. 8, lines 1 and 2: Hold both arms beseechingly, palms up. On ". . . set
me free . . ." open out arms wide. On ". . . from my . . . family
. . ." raise one arm, fist clenched to end.

24. I Love the Mountains

1. I love the moun-tains, I love the roll-ing hills, I love the dais-ies,
2. I love the green grass, I love the coun-try-side, I love the morn-ing,

I love the daf-fo-dils. I love the fire-side when all the lights are low.
bird songs at ev-en-tide. I love the sing-ing wind, blow-ing the sum-mer leaves.

*Chorus and Descant

Boom-de-a - da, Boom-de-a - da, Boom - de-a - da, Boom-de-a - da.

*Chorus can introduce the song and then act as descant for verses, as well as a chorus between verses.

3. I love the meadows, made for the heart of June,
I love the shadows dancing beneath the moon.
I love the whipoorwill close by my windowsill.

Chorus: Boom-de-a-da, Boom-de-a-da, Boom-de-a-da.

v. 1: On "mountains" raise one hand high. On "hills" make rolling motion. On "daisies, daffodils" hold both hands up, fingers curved slightly, not touching. On "fireside" hug yourself.

Chorus: Bang in rhythm with both fists alternately.

v. 2: On "grass" cast one arm out in a broad motion. On "countryside" the other arm the same. On "morning" yawn and stretch. On "bird songs" fly with one hand.

Chorus: as above.

v. 3: On "meadows" open both arms very wide. On "shadows" place hands over eyes. On "moon" make a circle over your head. On "whipoorwill" lock thumbs and fly.

Chorus: as above

25. I Point to Myself

I point to my - self, what have I here?

This is my top - notch - er, my dar - ling dear.

Top - notch - er, top - notch - er, my dar - ling dear,

That's what they taught me in school. Boom! Boom!

Verse	Point to	Sing
1.	head	topnotcher
2.	eye	eye winker
3.	brow	sweat browser
4.	nose	horn blower
5.	mustache	soup strainer
6.	mouth	bone crusher
7.	chin	chin chopper
8.	neck	rubber necker
9.	chest	chest sweller
10.	stomach	bread basket

On "boom, boom," slap each hand on thigh.

26. If You're Happy

2. If you're happy and you know it, stamp your feet;
   If you're happy and you know it, stamp your feet;
   If you're happy and you know it, then your face will surely show it;
   If you're happy and you know it, stamp your feet.

3. If you're happy and you know it, say amen;
   If you're happy and you know it, say amen;
   If you're happy and you know it, then your face will surely show it;
   If you're happy and you know it, say amen.

4.-100. *Make up some more!*

Clap once loudly after every time it says to do so, then do the other actions in the other verses. Try making up even more actions of your own.

27. I'm a Nut

1. I'm an a-corn, small and round, ly-ing on the cold, cold, ground. Peo-ple come and step on me; that's why I'm so cracked, you see. I'm a nut *(tsk! tsk!)* I'm a nut *(tsk! tsk!)* I'm a nut *(tsk! tsk!)* I'm a nut *(tsk! tsk!)* I'm a nut!

2. I'm so nut-ty, I don't know, why the squir-rels love me so. I'm de-scend-ed from an oak; nuts to you and that's no joke. I'm a nut *(tsk! tsk!)* I'm a nut *(tsk! tsk!)* I'm a nut *(tsk! tsk!)* I'm a nut *(tsk! tsk!)* I'm a nut!

v. 1: "I'm an acorn . . ." make a small hole with thumb and forefinger. At ". . . lying on the . . . ground . . ." tuck your face in against both hands held together. At ". . . step on me . . ." stomp once after phrase. At ". . . tsk, tsk . . ." rap knuckles against desk or or floor on these words.

v. 2: At "I'm so nutty . . ." make a face and stick out your tongue. At ". . . why the squirrels . . ." scurry up one arm with two fingers of the other hand. At "I'm descended from an oak . . ." hold elbow and wave that arm to and fro. At ". . . nuts to you . . ." make a face and stick tongue out. At ". . . tsk, tsk . . ." rap knuckles.

28. Itisket, Itasket

v. 1, lines 1 and 2: Slap both knees with hands on first beat of each measure. l. 3: Make writing motion. l. 4: Tap hands over your body
looking for letter.

v. 2: Hold head in hands and shake head from side to side. At "A
little boy . . ." hold hand low down, palm to ground, then put hand
in pocket.

Repeat first verse.

29. Jingle Bells

Dash-ing through the snow, in a one horse op - en sleigh;

O'er the fields we go, laugh-ing all the way.

Bells on bob - tail ring, mak - ing spir - its bright;

Oh, what fun it is to sing a sleigh-ing song to - night.

58

Hold reins and bounce up and down lightly in time throughout verse.

   Chorus: Make fist and shake it in time, as if ringing bells, and keep bouncing up and down (lightly).

30. Lavender's Blue

Lav - en - der's blue, Dil - ly, Dil - ly. Lav - en - der's green.

When I am king, Dil - ly, Dil - ly, You shall be queen.

Call up your men, Dil - ly, Dil - ly, set them to work, Some to the
Some to make hay, Dil - ly, Dil - ly, Some to cut corn, While you and

plow, Dil - ly, Dil - ly, Some to the farm.
I, Dil - ly, Dil - ly,
Keep our-selves warm.

line 1: Hold hands and sway from side to side.
  l. 2: "Call up your men . . ." make a beckoning motion.
  l. 3: ". . . set them to work . . ." point sharply.
  l. 4: "Some to the plow . . ." hold both hands out with fists closed.
  l. 5: "Some to make hay . . ." pitch hay.
  l. 6: Make cutting motion with hand.
  l. 7: "Keep ourselves warm . . ." hug yourself.

31. Little Bo-Peep

1. Lit - tle Bo Peep has lost her sheep, And can't tell where_ to find them. Leave them a - lone, and they'll come home, Wag - ging their tails,_ be - hind them.

2. Little Bo Peep, fell fast asleep,
   And dreamt she heard them bleating,
   But when she awoke, it was a joke,
   For they were still a-fleeting.

3. She sighed a sigh, and wiped her eye,
   And ran on hill and dale.
   She tried what she could to do some good,
   To tack each sheep to its tail.

v. 1, line 1: Shade your eyes with one hand. l. 2: "Leave them alone
. . ." make a dismissing motion with one hand by moving it
quickly from wrist outwards. l. 3: "Wagging their tails . . ."
wag *your* tail.

v. 2, lines 1 and 2: Close your eyes. l. 3 and 4: Wake up suddenly and
shade eyes.

v. 3, line 1: Sigh and wipe your eye. l. 2: Run up an arm with two fingers. l. 3: Hold up thumb and make "tack-on" motions in air.

Repeat verse 1.

32. Little Jack Horner

2. Little Jack Horner, sat in a corner,
   Eating his Christmas turkey.
   He lathered his hoss,
   With cranberry sauce,
   Because when he ran he was jerky.

3. Little Jack Horner, sat in a corner,
   Eating his Christmas stuffing.
   And then poor young Jack,
   He sat on a tack,
   Which left him huffing and puffing.

v. 1: Scrunch yourself up very small and eat.
       Stick in your thumb and pull out a plum.
       Pat yourself on the back.
v. 2: Scrunch again and eat again.
       Paint your horse.
       Make jerky motions with your body.
Repeat verse 1.

33. Little Peter Rabbit

Lit – tle Pet – er Rab – bit had a fly up-on his nose.

Lit – tle Pet – er Rab – bit had a fly up-on his nose.

Lit – tle Pet – er Rab – bit had a fly up-on his nose; He

flicked it and it flew a – way.

line 1: "Little Peter Rabbit . . ." hold first two fingers of one hand up, closing other fingers and waving the two.

l. 2: ". . . had a fly . . ." put pinky on nose.

l. 3: Repeat 1 and 2 twice, as words say.

l. 4: "He flicked it . . ." put forefinger on thumb and flick fly off nose, then move one hand away from yourself.

l. 5: Repeat the flick and the flying away motion.

For fun: Repeat song, dropping the last word in the verse each time, e.g., drop "nose," then sing again and drop "upon his," and continue that way, with rhythm and/or accompaniment continuing.

34. Little Rabbit Foo Foo

Lyrics under staff:

1. Lit - tle Rab - bit Foo - Foo, Hop-ping through the for - est,
2. Lit - tle Rab - bit Foo - Foo, I don't like your at - ti - tude,

(1. & 2.) Scoop-ing up the field mice, And bop-ping them on the head. *(to *)*
2. *(to **)*

*(*Spoken*) Down came the Good Fairy,
    And she said-- *(to 2.)*

**(*Spoken*) "I'll give you three chances,
    And if you don't behave,
    I'll turn you into a goon.
    The next day-- *(to 3.)*

3. Little Rabbit Foo-Foo,
    Hopping through the forest,
    Scooping up the field mice,
    And bopping them on the head.

    (*Spoken*) Down came the Good Fairy,
    And she said--

4. Little Rabbit Foo-Foo,
    I don't like your attitude,
    Scooping up the field mice,
    And bopping them on the head.

    (*Spoken*) "I'll give you two chances,
    And if you don't behave,
    I'll turn you into a goon.
    The next day--

5. Little Rabbit Foo-Foo,
    Hopping through the forest,
    Scooping up the field mice,
    And bopping them on the head.

    (*Spoken*) Down came the Good Fairy,
    And she said--

6. Little Rabbit Foo-Foo,
    I don't like your attitude,
    Scooping up the field mice,
    And bopping them on the head.

    (*Spoken*) "I'll give you one more chance,
    And if you don't behave,
    I'll turn you into a goon.
    The next day--

7. Little Rabbit Foo-Foo,
    Hopping through the forest,
    Scooping up the field mice,
    And bopping them on the head.

    (*Spoken*) Down came the Good Fairy,
    And she said--

8. Little Rabbit Foo-Foo,
    I don't like your attitude,
    Scooping up the field mice,
    And bopping them on the head.

    (*Spoken*) "I gave you three chances
    And you didn't behave.
    Now, I'll turn you into a goon!
    POOF!!!

The moral of the story is:

    HARE TODAY, GOON TOMORROW!

v. 1, line 1: Form rabbit with one hand by closing hand except for first two fingers, then "hop" with these two fingers through the air. l. 2: Make scooping motion with one hand cupped, then bop yourself on the head. l. 3: "Down came the good fairy . . ." raise one hand high and lower, waggling fingers.

v. 2, l. 1 and 2: Wag an admonishing finger, then scoop and bop as before. l. 2 and 4: "I'll give you three chances . . ." hold three fingers up. l. 5 and 6: "I'll turn you into a goon" point, then make a scary face.

v. 3 through 7: Repeat as before, except hold up two fingers on "two chances," and one finger on "one chance."

v. 8, l. 5: ". . . three chances . . ." hold up three fingers, then shake one finger critically. l. 8: On "Poof!" throw both arms out wide. At "Hare today" make a rabbit with two fingers. At "Goon tomorrow" make a scary face.

35. London Bridge

1. Lon - don Bridge is fall - ing down, Fall - ing down, fall - ing down.
2. Build it up with ir - on bars, Ir - on bars, ir - on bars.

Lon - don Bridge is fall - ing down, My Fair La - dy.
Build it up with ir - on bars, My Fair La - dy.

3. Iron bars will bend and break,
   bend and break, bend and break,
   Iron bars will bend and break,
   My Fair Lady.

4. Build it up with gold and silver,
   gold and silver, gold and silver,
   Build it up with gold and silver,
   My Fair Lady.

5. Send it to the USA,
   USA, USA,
   Send it to the USA,
   My Fair Lady.

6. That is where it is today,
   is today, is today,
   That is where it is today,
   My Fair Lady.

v. 1: Hold both arms up, wiggle fingers, and come down gradually; then repeat on second line.

v. 2: Push your hands up twice.

v. 3: Pretend to bend something with your hands and suddenly it breaks, as both hands "break." Repeat.

v. 4: Again push up twice with both hands.

v. 5: Point and repeat pointing through verse.

v. 6: Clap in rhythm.

36. Long-legged Sailor

1. Have you ev - er, ev - er, ev - er, in your long - leg - ged life, Seen a
2. Have you ev - er, ev - er, ev - er, in your short - leg - ged life, Seen a

long - leg - ged sail - or with a long - leg - ged wife?
short - leg - ged sail - or with a short - leg - ged wife?

3. Have you ever, ever, ever,
In your bow-legged life,
Seen a bow-legged sailor,
With a bow-legged wife?

4. Have you ever, ever, ever,
In your pigeon-toed life,
Seen a pigeon-toed sailor,
With a pigeon-toed wife?

5. Have you ever, ever, ever,
In your knock-kneed life,
Seen a knock-kneed sailor,
With a knock-kneed wife?

6. Have you ever, ever, ever,
In your cross-eyed life,
Seen a cross-eyed sailor,
With a cross-eyed wife?

7. Have you ever, ever, ever,
In your bald-headed life,
Seen a bald-headed sailor,
With a bald-headed wife?

8. Have you ever, ever, ever,
In your two-headed life,
Seen a two-headed sailor,
With a two-headed wife?

9. Have you ever, ever, ever,
In your frog-faced life,
Seen a frog-faced sailor,
With a frog-faced wife?

10. Have you ever, ever, ever,
In your bird-brained life,
Seen a bird-brained sailor,
With a bird-brained wife?

v. 1: Raise each leg one at a time and tramp in rhythm. On the words "long-legged sailor," point to any boy; on "long-legged wife," point to any girl.

v. 2: The same as above, but point to another boy and girl.

v. 3: Make your legs long by bending your knees down and outward slightly, then point again to a boy and girl.

v. 4: Make "pigeon toes" by pointing them inward toward each other, then point to a boy or girl.

v. 5: Knock your knees together, then point as before.

v. 6: Cross your eyes. The best way to do this is to stare at the bottom of your nose. Again point.

v. 7: Raise your head, and again point as above.

v. 8: Raise both fists, open and shut them and point.

v. 9: Make a "frog-face" by pressing the bottom of your nose upward; at the same time pull the underside of your eyes downward with your other hand. Point again.

v. 10: Make a silly face and point as above.

37. Michael Row the Boat Ashore

*1. Mich - ael, row the boat a - shore, Hal - le -
2. Sis - ter, help to trim the sails, Hal - le -

lu - jah; Mich - ael, row the boat a -
lu - jah; Sis - ter, help to trim the

shore, Hal - le - lu - jah.
sails, Hal - le - lu - jah.

*1st verse is also the chorus.

*Chorus:

    3. Jordan's river is deep and wide, Hallelujah;
       Milk and honey on the other side, Hallelujah.

Chorus:

    4. Jordan's river is chilly and cold, Hallelujah;
       Chills your body, but not your soul, Hallelujah.

Chorus:

v. 1: (This is also the chorus) Row in time to music.

v. 2: Make pulling motion with both hands from up to down alternately, one hand at a time.

v. 3: Open arms wide, then point to "the other side."

v. 4: Hug yourself and shiver, then shake your head "no." Do the chorus between each verse.

38. Mighty Pretty Motion

Chorus and Verse

1.Might-y pret-ty mo - tion, too - da-la, too - da-la, too - da-la.

Might-y pret-ty mo - tion, too - da-la, Rise, sug-ar, rise.

2. How-de-do Suzy,* toodala, toodala, toodala.
   How-de-do Suzy, toodala, Rise, sugar, rise.

3. Take off your heavy coat, toodala, toodala, toodala.
   Take off your heavy coat, toodala, Rise, sugar, rise.

4. Take off your heavy boots, toodala, toodala, toodala.
   Take off your heavy boots, toodala, Rise, sugar, rise.

5. Put on your overcoat, toodala, toodala, toodala.
   Put on your overcoat, toodala, Rise, sugar, rise.

6. Make something up, toodala, toodala, toodala.
   Make something up, toodala, Rise, sugar, rise.

v. 1: Wave your arms gracefully. Lift them up high on "rise, sugar, rise . . ."

v. 2: Bow to "Suzy," or use another name. Raise your arms as before.

v. 3: Pretend to remove coat. Or actually remove it if it is on you. Raise arms again on "rise . . ."

v. 4: Remove real or pretend boots or rubbers, then raise arms again.

v. 5, 6, etc.: Improvise verses and you can use verse 1 as a chorus between verses.

* *Name any name here.*

39. Miss Mary Mack

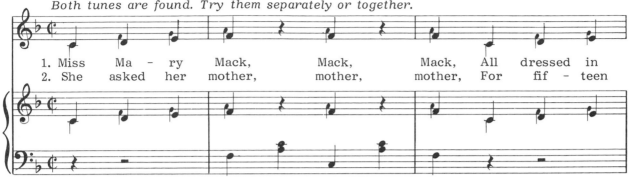

Both tunes are found. Try them separately or together.

1. Miss Ma - ry Mack, Mack, Mack, All dressed in
2. She asked her mother, mother, mother, For fif - teen

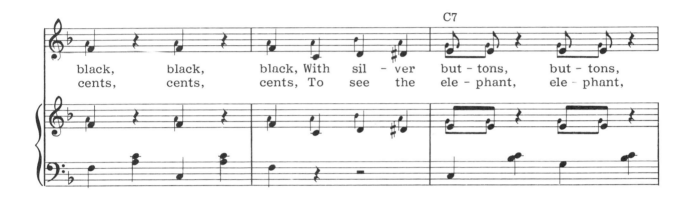

black, black, black, With sil - ver but - tons, but - tons,
cents, cents, cents, To see the ele - phant, ele - phant,

but - tons, All down her back, back, back.
ele - phant, Climb up the fence, fence, fence.

3. They jumped so high, high, high,
   They reached the sky, sky, sky,
   And never came back, back, back,
   Till the 4th of July, ly, ly.

4. She can not read, read, read,
   She can not write, write, write,
   But she can smoke, smoke, smoke,
   Her daddy's pipe, pipe, pipe.

5. She went upstairs, stairs, stairs,
   To make her bed, bed, bed,
   She made a mistake, stake, stake,
   And bumped her head, head, head.

6. Miss Mary Mack, Mack, Mack,
   All dressed in purple, purple, purple,
   With silver buttons, buttons, buttons,
   All down her girdle, girdle, girdle.

77

v. 1: Clap on the three "Macks," and clap on the three "blacks." Make a circle with thumb and forefinger and move that hand three times on the word "buttons." Slap your back thrice on the three "backs."

v. 2: Hold hand out, palm up, and go up and down with it three times on "mother," then touch finger of other hand in the palm three times on "cents." Then hold left hand out and make a "fence" with it by separating fingers, then climb fence with fingers of the right hand.

v. 3: Point your finger high three times each on the words "high," "sky," "back," and "July."

v. 4: Make a book of your hands, palms up, sides touching. Then shake your head "no." Keep shaking head "no" and make a writing motion with one hand. Then pretend to smoke a pipe.

v. 5: Climb in the air "upstairs" with two fingers. Pat a bed. Tap your head thrice on "mistake" and again three times on "head."

v. 6: Clap thrice on "Mack," and also on "purple." Make a circle with thumb and forefinger and move three times on "buttons" and on "girdle."

40. My Tall Silk Hat

One day_____ as I was rid - ing on the
went_____ and placed it on the seat be-

sub - way,_____ My tall silk hat,_____ My tall silk
side me,_____ My tall silk hat,_____ My tall silk

1.
hat._____ I

2.
hat._____ A

big_____ fat la - dy came and sat up - on it,_____ My tall silk

hat,＿＿＿＿＿ my tall silk hat.＿＿＿＿＿ A big＿＿＿＿＿

＿＿ fat la - dy came and sat up - on it,＿＿ My tall silk

hat,＿＿＿＿＿ It looked like that.＿＿＿＿＿

Christ - oph - er Co - lum - bo, Now what do you think of that?＿＿ A

big fat la – dy sat up-on my hat. My hat she

broke and that's no joke, My hat she broke and that's no joke;

Christ-oph-er Co-lum-bo, Now what do you think of that?____

l. 1: "One day as I was riding . . ." ride up and down. l. 2: "My tall silk hat . . ." put one hand on head and raise it way up. l. 3: ". . . on the seat beside me . . ." place hat beside you. l. 4: ". . . a big fat lady . . ." puff cheeks out and pat your belly. l. 5: ". . . sat upon it . . ." sit down heavily. l. 6: ". . . it looked like that . . ." with both hands describe something flattened out by placing one palm over the other. l. 7: "Christopher Columbo, now what do you think of that?" shake your fist in rhythm. l. 8: ". . . my hat she broke . . ." clap on "broke."

Note: Repeat actions when words repeat, e.g., shake fist in rhythm on last line, "Christopher Columbo . . .", as in 7.

41. One Finger, One Thumb

Keep adding things here, as verses proceed.

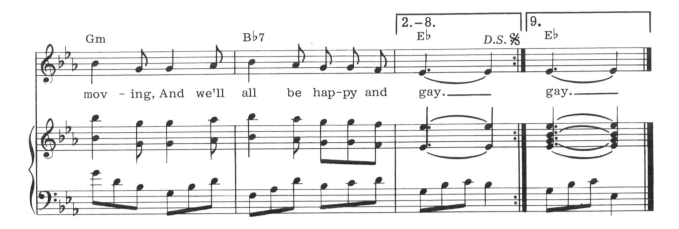

mov - ing, And we'll all be hap-py and gay._____ gay._____

3. One finger, one thumb, two hands, keep moving,
   One finger, one thumb, two hands, keep moving,
   One finger, one thumb, two hands, keep moving,
   And we'll all be happy and gay.

4. One finger, one thumb, one arm, keep moving,
   One finger, one thumb, one arm, keep moving,
   One finger, one thumb, one arm, keep moving,
   And we'll all be happy and gay.

5. One finger, one thumb, two arms, keep moving,
   One finger, one thumb, two arms, keep moving,
   One finger, one thumb, two arms, keep moving,
   And we'll all be happy and gay.

6. One finger, one thumb, one leg, keep moving,
   One finger, one thumb, one leg, keep moving,
   One finger, one thumb, one leg, keep moving,
   And we'll all be happy and gay.

7. One finger, one thumb, two legs, keep moving,
   One finger, one thumb, two legs, keep moving,
   One finger, one thumb, two legs, keep moving,
   And we'll all be happy and gay.

8. One finger, one thumb, get up, keep moving,
   One finger, one thumb, get up, keep moving,
   One finger, one thumb, get up, keep moving,
   And we'll all be happy and gay.

9. One finger, one thumb, sit down, keep moving,
   One finger, one thumb, sit down, keep moving,
   One finger, one thumb, sit down, keep moving,
   And we'll all be happy and gay.

Suit the action to the words. Note that the verses are "cumulative"; that is,
each preceding verse is repeated in subsequent verses.

42. Over in the Meadow

1. Ov - er in the mead-ow, in the sand, in the sun, Lived an
2. Ov - er in the mead-ow, when the sun had gone down, Then the

old moth - er toad,— and her lit - tle toad - ie one.
moon shone like sil - ver, on the green,— gras - sy ground.

"Wink," said the moth - er; "I wink," said the one; So they
"Grunt," said the moth - er; "I grunt," said the one; And they

winked and they blinked, in the sand, in the sun.
grunted and they grunted, when the moon chased the sun.

v. 1: Point to a meadow and then point down to sand. Make a sun with both hands in the air describing a circle. Hold up a fist for mother toad and a pinky for her "little toadie one." Wink when it says to and blink, and do that to end of verse.

v. 2: Point to meadow. Make the sun again and then lower the "sun." Make a moon overhead, same way, then grunt when it says to, keeping moon overhead to the end.

43. Polly Put the Kettle On

line 1: Hand in grasping position and place a kettle on fire. Do this three times. l. 2: Drink tea daintily; left hand is saucer; right hand holds cup to lips and down again on saucer. l. 3: Remove kettle three times, following words. l. 4: Throw both arms out wide, wiggling fingers, or waggling them, if you prefer, on ". . . they've all gone away."

44. Rabbit Ain't Got

1. Rab-bit ain't got no tail at all, tail at all, tail at all,
2. Tail__ is bare-ly there at all, there at all, there at all,

Rab-bit ain't got no tail at all, just a pow-der puff.*
Tail__ is bare-ly there at all, it ain't quite e - nough.**

* *Spoken:* Same song, 2nd verse-- A little bit louder and a little bit worse!

** *Spoken:* Same song, 3rd verse-- A little bit louder and a little bit worse!

   Chorus: Rabbit ain't got no tail at all, tail at all, tail at all,
          Rabbit ain't got no tail at all, just a powder puff.

Verse 3. Ears are longer than its tail, than its tail, than its tail,
          Ears are longer than its tail, just a piece of fluff.

   Chorus: Rabbit ain't got no tail at all, tail at all, tail at all,
          Rabbit ain't got no tail at all, just a powder puff.

 Spoken: Same song, 4th verse-- A little bit louder and a little bit worse!

    4. Repeat Verse 1.

Make a rabbit with one hand by closing hand except for first two fingers
which are held up and moved like rabbit ears. Shake heads "no" while doing
this, and on ". . . just a piece of fluff . . ." close hand completely. Repeat
all this in every verse.

45. Sarah the Whale

3. Now what would you do with a whale like that?
Now what would you do if she sat on your hat?
Or your tooth brush, or your mother,
Or anything that's helpless?
Spoken: Like that!!

v. 1: "In Frisco Bay . . ." describe circle horizontally before you with two hands. ". . . there lived a whale . . ." swimming motion with one hand. "They fed her oysters . . ." feed yourself. ". . . by tea-cup . . ." sip tea. ". . . by bathtub . . ." scoop up lots of oysters. ". . . and by schooner . . ." pull on ropes.

v. 2: ". . . when she smiled . . ." grin broadly, showing teeth. ". . . tonsils . . ." open mouth widely as possible. ". . . spareribs . . ." punch yourself in the ribs. ". . . too fierce . . ." look fierce.

v. 3: ". . . what would you do . . ." hold palms up and shrug. ". . . sat on your hat . . ." sit down hard. ". . . tooth brush . . ." scrub teeth. ". . . your mother . . ." point to a girl. "Like that!!" point to teacher.

46.   She Waded in the Water

lu - jah! Glo - ry, Glo-ry Hal-le-lu - jah! Glo - ry, Glo-ry Hal-le-

lu - jah! But she did-n't get her *(clap, clap)* wet, *(clap)* yet. *(clap)*

2. She waded in the water and she got her ankles all wet.
She waded in the water and she got her ankles all wet.
She waded in the water and she got her ankles all wet.
But she didn't get her *(clap, clap)* wet, *(clap)* yet. *(clap)*

Chorus: Glory, Glory, Hallelujah! Glory, Glory, Hallelujah!
But she didn't get her *(clap, clap)* wet, *(clap)* yet. *(clap)*

3. She waded in the water and she got her knees all wet.
She waded in the water and she got her knees all wet.
She waded in the water and she got her knees all wet.
But she didn't get her *(clap, clap)* wet, *(clap)* yet. *(clap)*

Chorus: Glory, Glory, Hallelujah! Glory, Glory, Hallelujah!
But she didn't get her *(clap, clap)* wet, *(clap)* yet. *(clap)*

4. She waded in the water and she got her thighs all wet.
She waded in the water and she got her thighs all wet.
She waded in the water and she got her thighs all wet.
But she didn't get her *(clap, clap)* wet, *(clap)* yet. *(clap)*

Chorus: Glory, Glory, Hallelujah! Glory, Glory, Hallelujah!
But she didn't get her *(clap, clap)* wet, *(clap)* yet. *(clap)*

5. She waded in the water and she finally got it wet.
She waded in the water and she finally got it wet.
She waded in the water and she finally got it wet.
She finally got her bathing suit wet.

v. 1: Stomp feet in rhythm, four times to a bar. Clap as indicated.
Chorus: Sing it and clap only where indicated.
v. 2: Slap ankles in rhythm; the rest as before.
v. 3: Slap knees similarly; the rest as before.
v. 4: Now the thighs; the rest as before.
v. 5: Like verse 1, but no chorus after the last verse.

47. Ten in a Bed

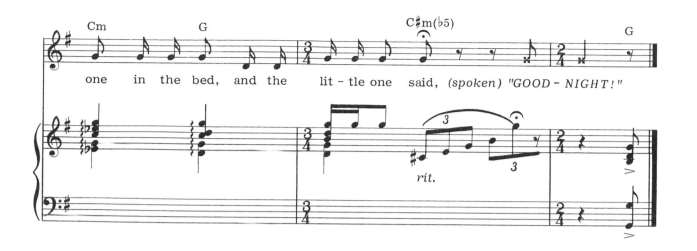

one in the bed, and the lit-tle one said, *(spoken)* *"GOOD - NIGHT!"*

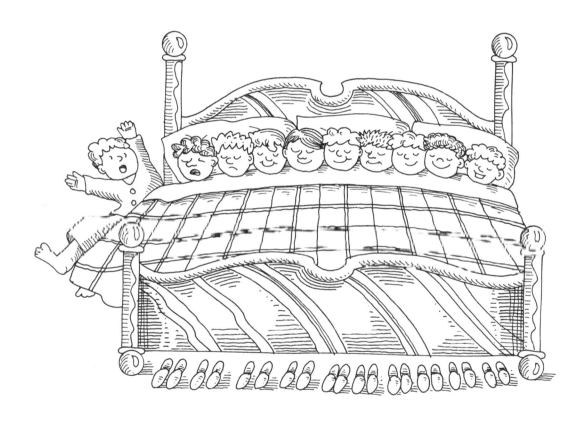

". . . ten in a bed . . ." hold up ten fingers. ". . . little one said . . ." bring thumb close together to forefinger but don't touch. "Roll over . . ." rolling motion with one finger making circles and moving from side to side. ". . . one fell out . . ." hold one finger up. ". . . nine in the bed . . ." hold nine fingers up, then roll. Do the same to the end, holding up one finger less each time, then on ". . . the little one said, 'Good-night!'" drop your head on chest and close your eyes. (No snoring!)

48. Three Craws

3. The second craw could not find his pa, find his pa, find his pa;
   The second craw could not find his pa, on a cold and frosty mornin'.

4. The third craw ate the other twa, the other twa, the other twa;
   The third craw ate the other twa, on a cold and frosty mornin'.

5. The fourth craw was not there at a', there at a', there at a';
   The fourth craw was not there at a', on a cold and frosty mornin'.

v. 1: Hold three fingers up and rest that hand on the other arm. Shiver on
". . . cold and frosty morning."
v. 2: Make a flying motion with right hand. Shiver again.
v. 3: Make a flying motion with left hand. Shiver again.
v. 4: With one hand grab two fingers of the other. Shiver.
v. 5: Shrug exaggeratedly. Shiver.

49. Three Little Angels

1. Three lit - tle ang - els all dressed in white,
2. Two lit - tle ang - els all dressed in white, . . . *simile*

tried to get to heav - en on the end of a kite. The

kite string broke and down they all fell; in -

stead of going to heav - en, they all went to--

(6 choruses)

Don't get ex - cit - ed, Don't get mis - lead, In -

stead of going to heav - en, they all went to bed!

3. One little angel all dressed in white,
   Tried to get to heaven on the end of a kite.
   The kite string broke and down they all fell;
   Instead of going to heaven, they all went to--

4. Three little devils all dressed in red,
   Tried to get to heaven on the end of a thread.
   The thread string broke and down they all fell;
   Instead of going to heaven, they all went to--

5. Two little devils all dressed in red,
   Tried to get to heaven on the end of a thread.
   The thread string broke and down they all fell;
   Instead of going to heaven, they all went to--

6. One little devil all dressed in red,
   Tried to get to heaven on the end of a thread.
   The thread string broke and down they all fell;
   Instead of going to heaven, they all went to-- *(to Coda)*

v. 1: "Three little angels . . ." hold three fingers up. ". . . end of a kite . . ." pull kite string. ". . . broke . . ." make a breaking motion with two fists twisting quickly in opposing movement. ". . . down they all fell . . ." bring one hand down with fingers waggling.

v. 2 and 3: Hold up appropriate number of fingers and then the same as above.

v. 4 through 6: For devils hold up a forefinger on either side of head as horns. The rest as before.

Coda: Wave head from side to side in rhythm. On "heaven," point upward; on "they all went to . . .", point downward.

50. Zum Gali Gali

103

Form partners. Song can be sung *a cappella* or piano can play the two voice parts. First voice part is the same throughout (ostinato). Children can sing both parts, or just voice one, while teacher sings second voice. The action: "Zum": touch palms to partner's palms, hands up. 2nd "Gali": slap partner's palm with one hand crossing, that is, right hand to right hand. 2nd "Zum": same as first. Last "Gali": slap left palm to left palm. This is done all through the song, which can take a lot of repetition.

ABOUT THE AUTHOR

Tom Glazer is one of the country's foremost balladeers. He started his career shortly after the great wave of "big-city" folk singing began, and performed often with Burl Ives, Leadbelly, Josh White, and others. His notable records for children include *Ballads for the Age of Science* and *On Top of Spaghetti*. He has appeared often in the theater and on leading radio and TV programs, many of which have won awards, notably his own recent show on station WQXR in New York. He is also a successful songwriter and composer, having written several hit songs and composed scores for TV and films. With Budd Schulberg he wrote songs and he composed the score for the Kazan-Schulberg, Warner Brothers film, *A Face in the Crowd*. He is the author of *Eye Winker, Tom Tinker, Chin Chopper, A New Treasury of Folk Songs* and *Tom Glazer's Treasury of Folk Songs for the Family*.